White Drawing Paper

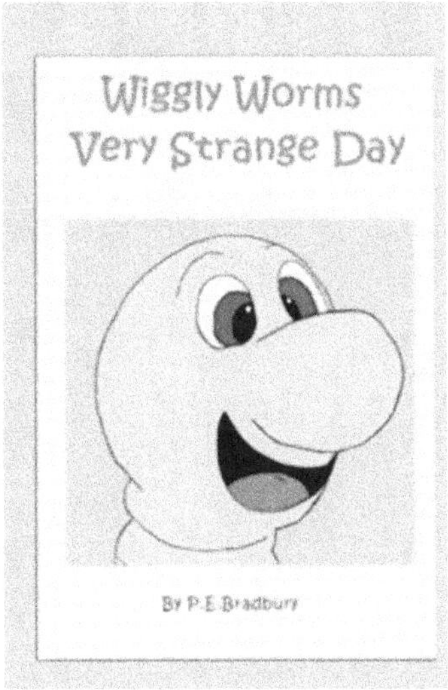

Brought to you by Paul E Bradbury,
author of "Wiggly Worms Very Strange Day",
also available on Amazon.com

www.ingramcontent.com/pod-product-compliance
Lightning Source LLC
Chambersburg PA
CBHW080538190526
45169CB00007B/2541
9781530536542